A PASSION FOR

OYSTERS

THE ART OF EATING AND ENJOYING

A PASSION FOR
OYSTERS

THE ART OF EATING AND ENJOYING

SHIRLY LINE

MITCHELL
BEAZLEY

Notes

Both metric and imperial measurements have been given in all recipes. Use one set of measurements only and not a mixture of both.

Standard level spoon measurements are used in all recipes.

Eggs should be size 3 unless otherwise stated.

Milk should be full fat unless otherwise stated.

Ovens should be preheated to the specified temperature - if using a fan assisted oven, follow the manufacturer's instructions for adjusting the time and the temperature.

Discard any oysters which are open before you come to eat or cook them, and any which do not open once cooked.

Art Director: **Jacqui Small**

Executive Art Editor: **Penny Stock**

Executive Editor: **Susan Haynes**

Editor: **Sasha Judelson**

Photography: **James Merrell**

Stylist: **Sue Skeen**

Home Economist: **Bridget Sargeson**

First published in Great Britain in 1995 by Mitchell Beazley,
an imprint of Reed Consumer Books Limited
Michelin House, 81 Fulham Road, London SW3 6RB
and Auckland, Melbourne, Singapore and Toronto

The moral rights of the author have been asserted.
Text copyright © Shirly Line 1995
Copyright © Reed International Books Limited 1995

The lines from Bernard Shaw's *Caesar and Cleopatra* are
reprinted with kind permission from The Society of Authors on behalf of the Estate of Bernard Shaw.

ISBN 1 85732 629 6
A CIP catalogue record for this book is available from the
British Library.

Produced by Mandarin Offset
Printed and bound in China

With great pleasure I dedicate this book to oyster lovers everywhere, and also to the oceans and seas around the world, the truly mighty forces who dictate the availability, size, nutritional value and beauty of this also mighty little mollusc.

CONTENTS

INTRODUCTION

There are two recognized oyster species: the *ostrea* and the *crassostrea*. To simplifiy, *ostrea* are mostly native oysters; whereas *crassostrea* have most commonly been introduced to the area.

Both oyster species have 'varieties' which belong to them. The smallest change in location or turn of the tide can affect the flavour, size and shape of any oyster and often when that happens, they change their name, so adding to the ever-growing list of oysters.

The *ostrea (edulis)* can be known as a European flat, Belon, Dorset or Whitstable. The Olympia oyster, well known in, and originally from America has the slightly different tag of *ostrea (lurida)*. On the east coast of the USA the *crassostrea (virginica)* is the dominant and native US oyster species; with the names Bluepoint, Louisiana and Chincoteagues being as well-known as peanut butter and Marilyn Monroe. Over on the west coast the *crassostrea (gigas)*, sometimes with the prefix of *Pacific*, takes over. They were originally imported from Japan in the early 1900s, as Portugese *crassostrea (angulata)*, to replenish emptied stocks of the Olympia.

APPEARANCES

Always buy oysters from a reputable supplier and check that the shells are tightly shut. A live and really fresh oyster uses the top and bottom muscles to hold the shell securely closed, especially when he hears somebody approaching with an oyster knife. When not feeling too well, the oyster will be too weak to hold tight the muscles and the shell will gape open - don't eat him or her - throw them away!

To open oysters easily, they may be heated in a preheated oven 200°C (400°F), Gas Mark 6, for about 5 minutes then plunged into iced water and drained. Alternatively, microwave them on High for about 20 seconds, depending on their size or prise the shells apart with an oyster knife.

Shelled oysters should be plump and sweet-smelling. The liquor (love potion) should be clear, and always used or drunk. To store oysters, please do not toss them into a bucket of water: they hate it and will die! Store with the deep cup down, in a refrigerator or cool, airy place: oysters need oxygen if they are alive.

Cover with a damp cloth or seaweed to prevent them from drying out and opening.

The temperature should be no higher than 4°C/34°F.

The old adage - that you should only eat oysters when there is an 'r' in the month - relates to *ostrea edulis* and arose because this species spawns in the summer months (May to August). Although there is nothing to stop you enjoying *edulis* oysters at this time, they are generally left to replenish stocks and anyway tend to be gritty and not very plump at this time. *Crassostrea* oysters do not spawn in their shells and are therefore available all year round; but they can be a little 'milky' when the weather is very warm.

BRITISH OYSTERS

There are quite a few oyster beds around the coastline of Great Britain and Ireland, and I have visited a number of them. Experience has taught me over the years that the finest flavour, shape and size must come from good husbandry. Oysters must be treated with loving care. I have seen farms that produce oysters looking like a bag of mis-shaped chocolates, and this is all due to their being left to grow under their own steam: no sorting and no turning to allow them space to breathe and to grow fatter. The following varieties and farms I can recommend as being the most caring in the business.

JERSEY OYSTERS - *HUÎTRES CREUSES*
(Crassostrea gigas)

The Royal Bay Oyster Company of Jersey was established in 1973, and names its bountiful catch after its very close neighbour, France.

Even though this beautiful island in the Channel Islands is so close to the vast French oyster industry, Royal Bay oysters can hold their own.

I was fascinated to see millions upon millions of oysters of various sizes housed in plastic netting sacks, spread along the east coast of the island at La Rocque near Grouville. I also learnt why Jersey oysters arrive at the market in such a perfect, slightly elongated shape, with a deep cup: this is because hour upon hour of work is put into the continuous turning of bags between the tides. Experts informed me that this was necessary to allow the live molluscs to move freely and to grow to a reasonable size within 3 years.

To my taste, the Jersey oysters were rather on the salty side, but the meat was a lively colour and rich in flavour due to feeding grounds where nutritious plankton is plentiful.

Is there any advantage for the Royal Bay Oyster Company in living so close to France? Of course there is. I spied with my own eyes sackloads of graded and washed freshly harvested oysters being loaded on to a boat for the west coast of France, to be grown on by one of the most popular oyster co-operatives. No, they won't be called Jersey oysters from Great Britain, they will be called French oysters; but then we are all one European Community now!

DORSET OYSTERS
(Ostrea edulis)

Today I consider the Dorset Native Oyster to be the *crème de la crème* of oysters. The demand for oysters from Poole Harbour is so great that the oysters do not have time to grow to more than 125 g/4 oz, and anyway it is unlikely that anyone would want to consume an oyster *au naturel* over this size. For consumption the most popular size for this little beauty is around 75-100 g/3-3½ oz when the sweetness of the pale and delicate meat is an experience never to be forgotten. This is not one for cooking.

So what makes a Dorset oyster so delicious? It must be something to do with the natural harbour in Poole, where the tidal rise and fall is only 2 m/6½ ft, due to a double high tide. This means that on warm, sunny days - and there are quite a few of these in the south of England - the shallow water warms quite quickly and the oysters can bask in the sun, feeding on the rich algae that gives them their special delicate flavour.

Dorset oysters are only available between the end of September and the end of April, those months which have an 'r' in them, thus allowing them to spawn in the warmer, summer months. They have a smooth, round, pale shell with a rather shallow base, and are easy to open, unlike some of the big *gigas* species. Dorset oysters are a wonderful and delicious once in a lifetime treat.

Apart from being found on the tables of top restaurants in Britain, Dorset oysters are sold in the plush hotels of Switzerland and Austria, where the cost does not count.

HELFORD OYSTERS - DUCHY OF CORNWALL

(Ostrea edulis and crassostrea gigas)

In the picturesque setting of Port Navas in Cornwall, Prince Charles, heir apparent to the English throne, owns oyster beds. Whether he displays the same emotion over his oyster stocks as he does for the plants at his Highgrove country home, information to date has not been leaked to the press, however it is confirmed that Prince Charles can produce over 2 million love potions a year out of the Helford river.

Oysters from the Duchy of Cornwall estate are superb in both quality and size; an area where the river meets the sea is reputed to be the best place for fattening oysters. Not to be too technical, it is known that the algae on which oysters thrive excel in these conditions, as when the Mississippi meets the Gulf waters in Louisiana to produce juicy, plump oysters. Bill Potter ('the oyster man') in Billingsgate tells of a customer who would have a special order of six 'Royales' from Helford, weighing 200-250 g/7-8 oz each, and who would tuck into them with a knife and fork direct from the shell, perhaps adding a few drops of Worcestershire sauce and a bread roll. That's big oyster talk, and true. Keith Floyd once described the Helford Duchy of Cornwall oysters as being 'sweet little dreams'.

Len Hodges, born and bred into the Prince's oyster beds and now the manager for Helford oysters, agrees with me that the finest flavour and quality come from the small No. 3s and 4s, and they certainly have a better texture. *Crassostrea gigas* are also farmed on the Helford River but do not compare in quality with the native *edulis*.

Helford oysters were polished and sent for the coronation of the Shah of Persia. The late Duke of Windsor had a huge passion for oysters which his mother, Queen Mary, fostered by ensuring that 300 Helford oysters were delivered to London every time he visited her. Perhaps the Duke of Windsor passed his love of oysters on to his nephew, Prince Charles?

COLCHESTER OYSTERS

(Ostrea edulis and Crassostrea gigas)

The oysters of Colchester are steeped in history. As far back as 1589, history relates to us that the most prestigious gift for the rich and noble of England would be succulent Colchester oysters.

Today, both native oysters (*ostrea edulis*) and *gigas* are farmed in the sheltered waters of England's east coast, sadly not in the vast quantities of years gone by, but the quality is still there. The native can be recognized by a pale roundish shell with a very shallow bottom shell. The *gigas* is big and rugged with a rather crinkly shell that can cut the hand on opening if a cloth does not guard it. These fellas are ideal for cooking because the meat has plenty of flavour and is firm when cooked.

BANNOW BAY OYSTERS

(Crassostrea gigas)

In 1614 Sir Caesar Colelough imported oysters from Milford Haven on the coast of Wales to the crystal clear waters of Bannow Bay on the eastern coast of Ireland. It soon became the finest oyster fishery in the country, and records in Tintern Abbey show that oysters from Bannow Bay were shipped regularly to court banquets in London and around Ireland. As this was at a time before the invasion of the *crassostrea gigas* oyster and before the disease bonamia hit so many of the oyster beds of Great Britain, one assumes that these were *ostrea edulis*, the native flat oysters.

Today, in the best tradition of oyster production and with modern techniques, *crassostrea gigas* are grown in the same crystal clear waters to produce a perfect gourmet delight. A deep cup shape with quite a crinkly edge to the shell, Bannow Bay oysters can be found throughout the year in a good medium size, and because the meat content is so fine with such a distinctive cool flavour, they are mostly eaten *au naturel* in Ireland, with just a light squeeze of lemon juice.

LOCH FYNE OYSTERS

(Crassostrea gigas)

Argyll in Scotland boasts a 96.5 km/60 mile long loch which is completely free from any pollution. Loch Fyne is a sea loch, fed by two rivers that make it the perfect feeding ground for oysters that are a little salty in taste, but which have a flavour so pure that they are not even subjected to the purification tanks required to be used by so many in the European Community. Loch Fyne Oysters have an oval shell with a deep cup. The company sells 800,000 oysters a year, not only in their own fine oyster bars, but also in large quantities to Hong Kong. The Chinese really enjoy Scottish oysters, describing them as 'big brains food'. A period of about 3 years is needed to produce a good size oyster in this vast loch. However, the grandfather of Loch Fyne is a *crassostrea gigas* oyster that has been around for 15 years and so will shortly be able to compete for a place in the *Guiness Book of Records*. Fondly known as Hamish, he must now weigh about 750 g-1 kg/1½-2 lb and has a craggy oval shell.

Pictured left

WEST MERSEA OYSTERS

(Ostrea edulis and Crassostrea gigas)

West Mersea native oysters first gained prominence for their quality and taste during the Roman occupation of Britain. The cultivation methods have not changed substantially for over a thousand years, ensuring that the flavour and quality of the oysters remains as in days long ago, although due to such a high demand some modern methods have been introduced to increase productivity. From August, West Mersea oysters are at a very saleable size, and where other varieties of oysters are still thin and tasteless, these oysters can be at a premium. Having been subjected to the latest ultra-violet cleaning process, the oysters can be found in many top London restaurants and are exported to Europe and the Far East. A distinguishing feature of the West Mersea *ostrea edulis* oyster is that the bottom shell is not quite as shallow as in most native *edulis* varieties. This has the advantage of being able to hold the precious love potion when opened. Since these are native oysters I would never cook them.

Pictured right

WHITSTABLE OYSTERS/SEASALTER SHELLFISH

(Crassostrea gigas)

These oysters are born in Whitstable, in algae-rich aerated sea water. A rapid growth to 3 mm/⅛ inch in diameter means the baby oysters can be transferred to the lagoon-fed nursery where they remain until large enough to be sold in Europe, or relaid in bags on the home ground to grow on for the English market. It takes 3 years of growth for the oysters to reach about 125 g/4 oz. When ready for market, they are purified in tanks for 48 hours. Their succulent richness in the summer months makes them perfect for cooking with meat or fish. Eat them *au naturel* and you will be reminded of a first dip in the ocean - natural, exciting, refreshing and shocking. An experience never to forget! Seasalter Shellfish Whitstable offer a very efficient postal service for oysters delivered to anywhere in Britain and they will always arrive on time, in perfect condition.

Pictured left

ISLAY OYSTERS

(Crassostrea gigas)

Islay oysters are grown on a small island off the west coast of Scotland which benefits from a mild marine climate, while its waters are warmed by the Gulf Stream. They are grown in a sea loch which experiences very strong tides and has excellent feeding. The tide has to race over 4.8 km/3 miles of sandy bottom to reach the dedicated trestles, during which time it warms considerably. Such excellent marine conditions mean quick-growing oysters, which seem to be in peak condition all the year round.

The oysters from Islay are some of the creamiest oysters you could hope to taste and are much sought after by connoisseurs.

I have learnt never to mix strong spirits with the delicate oyster, but Japanese visitors to the Island of Islay do indulge in both, especially when they can try the famous malt whiskies - Bowmore, Laphroaig and Lagavullin - which are part of the island's heritage.

Pictured right

SEACROFT OYSTERS
(*Crassostrea gigas*)

Seacroft oysters are farmed in West Loch Tarbert, a sheltered sea loch at the head of the Kintyre peninsula, where the oysters can benefit from the warm and shallow seas.

Neil Duncan, who farms at West Loch, has developed a unique system for suspending his nets of oysters in the water, which ensures that each animal has unrivalled access to constant feeding.

With such loving care and attention, it is no wonder that these oysters are highly sought after in Britain and on the Continent. They have an excellent meat content, with just the right amount of creaminess and are perfect to consume on the shell with a squeeze of lemon juice, or for cooking.

Seacroft oysters are available all year round.

Pictured right

CAREW OYSTERS
(*Crassostrea gigas*)

The long stretch of Cleddau Estuary in Pembrokeshire, south Wales is the most famous oyster bed serving not only Wales but also Herefordshire and Worcestershire, with a fresh supply of oysters all the year round. Perhaps it is the rich variety of river life combined with the run-off from agricultural land, the salt marsh and the limestone quarries that put so much goodness and flavour into these perfect Welsh oysters. Added to this is the perfectly balanced mix of minerals, which always occurs when the river meets the sea, and which means that the oysters are certain to grow well.

The succulent meat of the Carew oyster has such a richness and perfect balance of saltiness that it has been described as 'a peach of the seas'. Carew oysters may be eaten on the shell with a squeeze of lemon, or used for cooking. They are ideal for both, whatever the size.

Pictured left

ORKNEY SEAFAYRE OYSTERS
(Crassostrea gigas)

The Orkney Isles off the coast of the Scottish Highlands must be the perfect place for growing oysters. Clear, pure unpolluted waters produce an oyster with a very clean shell that is a pretty pale colour with just a hint of the blue sea. The flavour is quite salty and very often is compared to a French *crues*. A deep-bottomed shell makes the Orkney Seafayre oyster ideal for using when a recipe advises serving 'in a shell'.

A super and yet simple recipe involves poaching the oysters lightly in orange juice, then mixing eggs, breadcrumbs, snipped chives and finely grated orange rind in a saucepan and heating gently until the eggs are cooked. The drained oysters are then folded into the mixture, returned to the deep shells and cooked under a hot grill for 2 minutes until the breadcrumbs are crisp.

Pictured right

ROSSMORE IRISH OYSTERS
(Ostrea edulis and Crassostrea gigas)

Commercially recognised as Rossmore oysters, Atlantic Shellfish from Cork Harbour on the Irish west coast must offer some of the most perfect conditions for oysters: a sheltered, shallow, warm breeding ground with the run-off from the richest agricultural area of Ireland.

Atlantic Shellfish produce both species of oyster: the native *ostrea edulis* and the *crassostrea gigas*, also known as the Rock oyster. Rock oysters can be found all the year round, not only in Britain but also most countries in Europe, and in many prestigious restaurants. I firmly believe Rossmore Rock oysters have the highest meat content of any oyster grown in Europe. The ones I had were super and not too salty - perfect for cooking in the shell, in a casserole or thrown on the barbecue. The native oysters are beautiful with an iridescent blueness to the shells. The Rock oysters have a very deep golden shell of perfect shape. Constant turning during cultivation stops them from growing bent and flat.

Pictured left

OYSTER CURIOSITIES

The Aphrodite Inheritance

Oysters have always been linked with love. When Aphrodite, the Greek goddess of love, sprang forth from the sea on an oyster shell and promptly gave birth to Eros, the word 'aphrodisiac' was also born.

Richly laden tables of asparagus, snails and ostrich brain were dictated as the staple diet for the infamous Roman orgies from around 5 BC; with no great feast being complete without the prized delights for lust and pleasure: oysters.

Around AD 76, the Roman Emperor Vitellus, famed for eating oysters continuously throughout the day and night, ordered thousands of slaves to gather native oysters (*ostrea edulis*) from the south coast of England. He had the oysters transported to Rome to feed emperors and guests alike; never before had such a humble living creature aroused such passionate feelings. Vitellus preferred oysters to grapes, while the ladies of the court enjoyed their oysters most of all when dipped in honey.

The history of the oyster is rich with subtle and pleasurable nuances; although Aristotle thought the oyster to have 'no sensation of sex', Apuleius, famed for his work *The Golden Ass*, written in AD 125, reputedly made a love potion of oysters with which to seduce Aemilia, and look what oysters did for Casanova. It is said that he consumed up to about 60 oysters a day. Oysters are the ideal food to replace the lost zinc needed to improve male fertility. British men should follow the legendary Italian lover and eat more oysters. American health guidelines suggest that 15 mg of zinc should be included in the male diet; the British average is only 8 mg and less.

Pharmacologically the true aphrodisiac capacity of an oyster really depends on the dopamine content. This is a vital neurotransmitter which helps to govern brain activity and influence sexual desire. Dopamine provokes sexual interest and triggers responses, while improving performance in both males and females. It is said to amplify the intensity of sensation.

Health and Nutrition

Often posed questions include: Are oysters good for you? Do oysters improve your health? One thing is for sure, with approximately 75 calories in 12 oysters and a guarantee that they will improve your sex life, a dozen to replace a meal twice a day for a week could have the most fantastic results!

All fish and shellfish contain natural polyunsaturated oils - known as Omega 3 fatty acids - recognized by medical experts as fundamental for good health. These essential fish oils play a role in maintaining clear arteries, and are also of benefit to the central nervous system. It is true that the bigger and fatter the oysters the bigger the helping of Omega 3, but these oils are now regarded as of more benefit than risk for those suffering with a little too much cholesterol.

When asked why he ate oysters in a restaurant when he adhered to Jewish dietary laws and shunned shellfish in his home a charming 98 year old Jewish gentleman declared: 'I only indulge in my three dozen oysters a week at the Oyster Bar because my doctor recommends them for a long life and happy heart'. Indeed, a 50 g/2 oz oyster could soon be rocking the salted peanut from his stool at the café, pub, cocktail bar, bistro or tapas bar.

Nutritional Values

Oysters contain the following: Vitamins: A, B1, B2, C and D; Minerals include: Calcium, Iodine, Magnesium, Iron, Potassium, Copper, Sodium, Zinc, Phosphorus, Manganese and Sulphur. Forget the vitamin and mineral pills, just eat a dozen oysters! On very rare occasions, oysters may contain harmful microbes. The American Food and Drug Administration estimates that 5 per cent of shellfish, including oysters, contain *vibrio vulnificus* bacteria, which could cause people suffering from allergies, diabetes, AIDS or other diseases to become quite ill. Cooking kills the bacteria, as does serving them with a hot spicy sauce (according to a research team at Louisiana State University). Dr Charles Saunders told the New York Times: 'I still eat plenty of oysters, but I do like my hot sauce'.

The biggest concern with all shellfish remains just how long it has been hanging around. Wherever, whatever, buy your oysters from a reputable fishmonger and when eating out, choose a restaurant known for the freshness of its fish and the rapidity of its turnover.

History

Oysters have been an important food since Neolithic times. They were cultivated in China before the Christian era, the Greeks served them with wine and the Romans were so enthusiastic about these marvellous molluscs that they sent thousands of slaves to the shores of the English channel to gather oysters. English oysters were so highly prized by Roman generals that they paid for them by their weight in gold. The biggest expense, however, as it is today, was the cost of transportation across the sea and then over the Alps. The oysters were packed in snow-covered barrels to keep them alive during transportation.

The native Americans were great lovers of the oyster too, as is evidenced by the millons of shells which archeologists have discovered. When the Indians of North America got hooked on oysters four thousand years ago, they felt it too cannibalistic to eat the creatures alive; so they invented oyster stew.

Oysters were an important - and inexpensive - part of the diet in Britain from the Middle Ages through to the 19th century. It was estimated that 700 million oysters a year were eaten in London alone in 1864. Chaucer, Shakespeare, Byron and Charles Dickens extolled the virtues of the oyster. Pepys' Diary contains several references, including a description of a New Year's breakfast which featured a barrel of oysters. By the end of the 19th century, however, oysters had become rarer and much more costly, due to increasing demand and overdredging of the natural oyster beds, and plans were put in motion for the establishment of the first British artifical oyster beds.

In 1910 the USA led the world in terms of oyster yields with 26,800,000 bushels, with France lying in second place with 3,250,000 bushels. From Texas to Cape Cod, overharvesting and uncontrollable diseases have depleted the stocks of years gone by. The good news today must be that after a lapse in oyster production, due to problems of pollution, over-fishing and disease, not only in America, but also in Great Britain and other European countries, things are picking up. The future could be something to really cheer about, and the famous oyster opening competition in St Mary's County Oyster Festival, Maryland, could be bigger than ever.

Oysters commence life as male, and then decide after 12 months that they prefer to be female. Although a rich diet and warm waters dictate that oysters remain female, the female oyster likes to revert back to being male after spawning. The male oyster also goes through the process of childbirth, laying as many as 1 million eggs a year, just like the female oyster.

SERVING OYSTERS

In France, oysters are served on a large platter of crushed ice. The oysters are left in the shell with the bottom muscle uncut, and still attached to the shell, to allow the customer to see that they are fresh. In Britain they are served with the top muscle cut, the top shell discarded and the bottom muscle also cut to allow the oyster to be turned in the shell before serving - because the British feel that this is a prettier sight.

Do not cook with tiny oysters, if cooked they shrivel down to become tiny black spots and will lose much of their original taste.

For a dinner party allow 6 fresh oysters per person and serve on individual plates of crushed ice. Select oysters of a similar size. Open them just before serving, removing the top shell. Serve with oyster forks and wedges of lemon.

It is not true that you eat the oyster alive because immediately the shell is prised apart and oxygen enters, the oyster will die; and with a squeeze of lemon he/she will have the last wriggle.

WHAT TO DRINK WITH OYSTERS

Champagne is a must if the oysters are of the native species (*ostrea edulis* or European flats). Oz Clarke once wrote that he felt the champagne was more of an aphrodisiac than the oyster. Buck's Fizz (a mixture of orange juice and champagne) would be wonderful if serving oysters for breakfast or brunch.

If you indulge in oysters in Ireland or at a party where the host is Irish, no doubt you will be treated to wonderful Black Velvet (champagne and Guinness).

It is not really necessary to serve an expensive white wine with oysters. If the wine is exceptional, it will take the whole show away from the oysters. A bottle of Muscadet is a choice with which you cannot go far wrong. I used to enjoy French, Californian or Australian Chardonnay, in particular the rich woody flavour of the Napa family or Australian range, but again I think I would prefer something to drink that is not as distinctive in taste; do not forget the seaweedy, salty, mineral taste that the wine will have to compete with.

A copita of Spanish dry sherry taken straight from the refrigerator is perfect with all shellfish, especially oysters.

A word of warning: never drink whisky, brandy or other strong spirits with or after eating oysters. They react together in the stomach and will both be rejected in quite an unpleasant way.

THE RECIPES

Oysters *au naturel* are best served simply, with crushed ice and seaweed, samphire or salsify. Fresh lemon juice or Worcestershire sauce are both good accompaniments. A connoisseur will tell you that Tabasco is too strong and will kill the delicate flavour of a good oyster. There are 2 classic sauces to be served with oysters. The first is mignonnette sauce, a combination of 1 chopped shallot, juice of ½ a lemon, 6 tablespoons of red wine vinegar and freshly ground black pepper. The second, chilli sauce, is a variation on mignonette sauce. Make as above with the addition of 2 deseeded and finely chopped green chillies, 4 sprigs of coriander, finely chopped and a pinch of sugar. Both sauces should be kept refrigerated. Fresh oysters may be frozen for up to 3 months. Do not remove them from the freezer within 24 hours of freezing. Allow 55 minutes to thaw and then serve immediately.

ANGELS ON HORSEBACK

This simple and tasty recipe for oysters was made popular in the reign of Queen Victoria and has been a popular savoury in Great Britain ever since. When oysters were not available, scallops were used instead and the recipe appeared on the menu as *Archangels on Horseback*. I have never been able to understand where the business of 'horses' came in and am still waiting to find out!

Open as many Pacific oysters as you will need, reserving the liquor. Wrap each oyster in a rasher of streaky bacon and secure with a wooden cocktail stick. Cook under a fairly hot grill or on the barbecue, turning until the bacon is crispy. Remove from the grill or barbecue and then roll in a generous amount of fine fried breadcrumbs or place on crisp warm toast, before serving with a garnish of watercress.

Or try *The Poacher's Breakfast*, a recipe created by the oyster dredgers of the English Kent coast over 50 years ago. The working men would always sneak a few oysters into their pockets while out at sea. Breakfast on board the oyster smack would consist of the forbidden fruit concealed in streaky bacon and then fried in bacon dripping with a couple of eggs cracked in the pan for good measure.

'But four young Oysters hurried up,
All eager for the treat:
Their coats were brushed, their faces washed,
Their shoes were clean and neat–
And this was odd, because, you know,
They hadn't any feet'.

Lewis Carroll *Alice Through the Looking Glass*

OYSTER AND CAVIAR CANAPÉS

as much caviar as you can afford

8 oysters - Dorset native oysters (*ostrea edulis*)

juice of 1 lemon

freshly ground black pepper

finely chopped parsley, to garnish

2 lemons, quartered, to serve

Tartlet Shells

175 g/6 oz plain flour

25 g/1 oz lard

50 g/2 oz butter

pinch of salt

6-7 tablespoons iced water

Make the tartlet shells. Put the flour in a mixing bowl, cut in the fats and rub them in until the mixture resembles fine breadcrumbs. Add the salt, then mix in the water a little at a time until the mixture forms a firm dough. Wrap the pastry in clingfilm and allow it to rest in the refrigerator for 30 minutes.

Preheat the oven to 190°C (375°F), Gas Mark 5. Roll out the pastry thinly on a lightly floured surface to line 8 greased round or boat-shaped moulds, measuring about 6 cm/2½ inches. Prick the pastry all over with a fork, line with nonstick baking paper and fill with dried or pastry beans. Bake blind for 10 minutes.

Remove the paper and beans then carefully remove the pastry shells and leave to cool on a wire rack. Just before serving, divide the caviar equally between the cooled pastry shells. Open the oysters, reserving the liquor for use in another recipe. Top each caviar-filled pastry shell with an oyster and sprinkle lightly with lemon juice. Garnish with parsley and serve with lemon wedges. Offer a pepper mill at the table.

Serves 4

OYSTER CHOWDER

300 g/10 oz lean pork, cut into bite-sized pieces

1 onion, chopped

3 celery sticks, diced

1 green pepper, deseeded and diced

4 potatoes, diced

300 ml/½ pint fish stock

600 ml/1 pint milk

24 big oysters (anything but native *ostrea edulis* or **Belons**)

juice of 1 lemon

3 tablespoons plain flour

50-75 g/2-3 oz butter, softened

250 ml/8 fl oz Noilly Prat or dry white cinzano

12 small clams (in their shells, shells scrubbed)

salt and pepper

paprika, to garnish

Heat the pork gently in a pan until the fat runs, raise the heat, add the onion and sauté for 3 minutes. Add the celery, green pepper, potatoes and fish stock, cook for 3 minutes, then stir in the milk, season to taste. Bring to the boil and simmer until the pork cubes and vegetables are cooked through. Open the oysters, adding the liquor to the pan with the lemon juice. In a small bowl, mix the flour and butter to a paste; add a small amount at a time to the simmering liquid in the pan, stirring thoroughly each time, until the sauce thickens. Stir in the Noilly Prat or dry cinzano. Add the clams and fold in the oysters. Simmer for 2 minutes so the clams open. (Discard any that remain shut.) Serve with a sprinkling of paprika.

Serves 4-6

OYSTER AND GUINNESS SOUP

Do not use too big an oyster for this soup; medium-sized Pacific (*gigas*) are ideal.

125 g/4 oz butter

I onion, chopped

150 ml/¼ pint dry white wine

50 g/2 oz plain flour

300 ml/½ pint fish stock or court bouillon

24 oysters

300 ml/½ pint Guinness

150 ml/¼ pint double cream

salt and pepper

plenty of finely chopped parsley, to garnish

Melt 50 g/2 oz of the butter in a saucepan, add the onion and fry until softened. Pour in the wine, bring to simmering point and simmer for 3 minutes.

Meanwhile melt the remaining butter in a separate pan, stir in the flour and cook for I minute. Gradually add the fish stock or court bouillon, stirring constantly until you have a creamy sauce to add to the wine and onions. Mix well, then add salt and pepper to taste.

Open the oysters, adding the liquor to the soup. Pour the Guinness into the soup and stir constantly until it reaches boiling point. Reduce the heat to low, stir in the cream and then fold in the oysters with loving care. Continue to cook over a low heat for I minute only before serving in heated soup bowls.

Garnish with chopped parsley.

Serves 4-6

OYSTER 'CHIPS'

These make an excellent savoury lunch-time snack.

36 medium oysters

oil, for deep frying

Batter

50 g/2 oz plain flour

2 eggs, beaten

300 ml/½ pint milk

grated nutmeg

salt and pepper

Place the oysters in a large heavy-bottomed saucepan over a moderate heat. Cover the pan tightly and steam the oysters, shaking the pan frequently, until they open. Discard any that remain shut. Drink the oyster liquor or reserve it for use in another recipe. Remove the oysters from the shells and pat them dry with kitchen paper. Set aside.

Make the batter. Mix the flour and eggs in a bowl. Gradually beat in the milk until the mixture forms a smooth coating batter. Add nutmeg, salt and pepper to taste.

Gently drop the oysters into the batter, carefully rolling them around until they are evenly coated.

In a large, deep saucepan, heat the oil for deep frying to 180-190°C (350-375°F), or until a cube of bread added to the oil browns in 30 seconds. Fry the battered oysters, one at a time. Each oyster takes only a few seconds - it will only take 1 minute to cook all 36 oysters, give or take a few seconds. Using a slotted spoon transfer the cooked oysters to kitchen paper to drain, then pile into a warm serving dish and serve at once.

Makes 36

MARINATED OYSTERS AND SALMON

This is highly suitable as an hors d'œuvre. Use a medium-sized oyster with a firm meat content, which is not too salty. *Crassostrea gigas* or *virginica* oysters are ideal. Because the salmon is not cooked, it is important that it be fresh and from a reputable source.

24 oysters

500 g/1 lb fresh salmon fillet

Marinade

300 ml/½ pint dry white wine

6 tablespoons fresh orange juice

2 tablespoons soy sauce

1 tablespoon sugar

12 drained capers

salt and pepper

Garnish

1 kiwifruit, sliced (optional)

3-4 radicchio leaves, shredded

Prepare the marinade at least 1½ hours before you want to serve this dish. Combine all the marinade ingredients in a saucepan and bring to the boil. Remove from the heat and set aside to cool slightly. Open the oysters, adding the liquor to the marinade. Remove the oysters from their shell and place them on a flattish dish.

Trim the salmon and cut it into pieces the same size as the oysters. Arrange the pieces on the dish with the oysters and spoon the warm marinade over both. Leave until cold, then cover and chill in the refrigerator for 1 hour. Garnish with kiwifruit, if using and shredded radicchio leaves and serve.

Serves 6

OYSTER AND PUMPKIN SOUFFLÉS

This unusual combination makes an impressive starter. Use small, flavoursome oysters.

50 g/2 oz butter, plus extra for greasing

12 oysters

25 g/1 oz plain flour

300 g/10 oz finely mashed cooked pumpkin

pinch of cayenne pepper

4 eggs, separated

pinch of grated nutmeg, or to taste

salt and pepper

watercress to garnish (optional)

At least 1 hour in advance grease four 10 cm/4 inch ovenproof ramekins and place them on a baking sheet in the freezer (this allows the soufflés to come away from the sides with ease). Preheat the oven to 200°C (400°F), Gas Mark 6. Open the oysters, reserving the liquor.

Melt the butter in a saucepan over a gentle heat, stir in the flour and cook for 1 minute. Add the mashed pumpkin and reserved oyster liquor, stirring constantly until thoroughly mixed. Add the cayenne, with salt and pepper to taste. Remove the pan from the heat and stir in the egg yolks, one at a time. Return to a low heat and stir constantly until the mixture thickens a little more and is smooth.

Whisk the egg whites in a grease-free bowl until stiff; gently fold them into the pumpkin mixture using a metal spoon. As soon as the mixture is blended, spoon it into the prepared ramekins. Drop 3 oysters into each dish and dust with a little nutmeg.

Bake the soufflés for 20-25 minutes, until the tops are firm and golden. Serve immediately, garnished with watercress, if using; and don't wait for any late arrivals!

Serves 4

OYSTERS ROLAND JÖHRI - ST MORITZ

This special dish is made in 2 stages, the recipe for the pasta shavings on which the oyster shells rest is on page 63. The pasta should be prepared first.

16 Dorset native oysters (*ostrea edulis*)

4 tablespoons whipped cream or crème fraîche

1 tablespoon Noilly Prat or dry white Cinzano

2 tablespoons Chardonnay

1 egg yolk, beaten

pinch of saffron

25 g/1 oz butter

10 leaves of young fresh spinach, cut into strips

grated nutmeg, to taste

salt and pepper

Open the oysters reserving the liquor in a pan. Set the oysters aside and scrub the bottom shells. Bring a saucepan of water to the boil, add the bottom shells and boil for 10 minutes. Drain and set aside.

Add 2 tablespoons of the whipped cream or crème fraîche to the oyster liquor, together with the Noilly Prat or Cinzano and the Chardonnay. Boil until reduced by half. Remove from the heat and stir in the beaten egg yolk, saffron and remaining cream or crème fraîche.

Melt the butter in a frying pan, add the spinach and toss lightly until just tender. Season with nutmeg, salt and pepper. Toss the spinach with the pasta and spoon on to a large platter.

Arrange the oyster shells on the pasta mixture, return the oysters to their shells, and cover each oyster with the sauce. Pop under a hot grill for just a few seconds, to warm the oysters.

Serves 4

BARLEY SALAD WITH OYSTERS

16 Belon oysters

fresh lemon juice

finely snipped chives, to garnish

endive or lambs' lettuce, to serve

Barley Salad

50 g/2 oz Scotch or pot barley, soaked overnight in water to cover and drained

50 g/2 oz small courgettes, cut into small pieces

50 g/2 oz baby carrot, cut into small pieces

50 g/2 oz spring onions, cut into small pieces

I large tomato, skinned, seeded and cubed

Sherry Dressing

2 tablespoons sherry vinegar

2 tablespoons Dijon mustard

I tablespoon sherry

4 tablespoons cold pressed extra virgin olive oil

pinch of sugar

salt and pepper

Add the barley to a pan of boiling water and simmer for I hour or until tender. Drain and allow to cool. Mix the barley with all the salad vegetables. For the dressing, mix together the vinegar, mustard and sherry. Whisk in the oil, add sugar, salt and pepper to taste. Open the oysters, adding the liquor to the dressing. To serve, pour the dressing over the barley and vegetables, mix well. Divide the salad between 2 plates and top each with 8 oysters, adding lemon juice. Garnish with chives and endive or lambs' lettuce.

Serves 2

CHILLI GRILLED OYSTERS MEXICO WAY

Use an oyster which has a deep cup, such as the Rock oyster from Cork Harbour, or the
Portuguese oyster.

12 oysters

I red chilli, deseeded and sliced, or chilli paste to taste

I cm/½ inch piece of fresh root ginger, peeled and finely chopped

4 tablespoons fresh breadcrumbs

50 g/2 oz butter, softened

2-4 tablespoons Bacardi or white rum

sea salt (see method)

Open the oysters, reserving the liquor. Set the oysters aside and scrub the bottom shells. Bring a
saucepan of water to the boil, add the bottom shells and boil for 10 minutes. Drain and set aside.
Using a pestle, pound the chilli with the ginger in a mortar until smooth. Gradually mix in the breadcrumbs and reserved oyster liquor. Spoon the mixture into a bowl and stir in the butter until thoroughly
mixed. Add enough of the rum to make a spreadable mixture.

Cover a baking sheet with sea salt to hold the oyster shells without tipping. Return the oysters to the
shells and cover each one with the chilli crumb mixture. Place the filled shells carefully on the salt-topped
baking sheet and cook under a very hot grill for about 2 minutes or until the breadcrumbs are
nicely toasted. Serve at once.

Serves 4

OYSTER AND BEEF PÂTÉ

25 g/1 oz butter

12 Pacific (*gigas*) oysters

175 g/6 oz finely minced lean beef

50 g/2 oz green pepper, deseeded and finely chopped

1 shallot, finely chopped

1 teaspoon tomato purée

2 eggs, beaten

50 g/2 oz fresh breadcrumbs

salt and pepper

Garnish

50 g/2 oz butter

250 g/8 oz fresh mushrooms or drained canned mushrooms, sliced

1 garlic clove, chopped

watercress

Preheat the oven to 180°C (350°F), Gas Mark 4. Using the butter, generously grease 4 ovenproof ramekins. Open the oysters, reserving the liquor in a bowl. Remove the oysters, chop coarsely and add to the liquor together with the beef, green pepper and shallot. Mix well, and stir in the tomato purée, beaten eggs and breadcrumbs. Mix thoroughly, add salt and pepper to taste. Divide the mixture between the ramekins. Place in a roasting pan, pour in boiling water to 2.5 cm/1 inch from the ramekin tops. Bake for 20 minutes.

Just before serving, prepare the garnish. Melt the butter in a pan over a gentle heat, add the mushrooms and garlic and toss lightly until tender. Remove the ramekins from the *bain-marie*. Turn out on to 2 plates. Spoon half the mushroom mixture around each pair of pâtés and garnish with watercress. Serve at once.

Serves 2

BAKED OYSTERS AUSTRALIAN STYLE

The baked oysters can be prepared before guests arrive and served just warm.

25 g/1 oz unsalted butter

2 garlic cloves, crushed

175 g/6 oz fresh wholemeal breadcrumbs

75 g/3 oz blue vein cheese, grated or crumbled

48 large Pacific (*gigas*) oysters

150 ml/¼ pint soured cream

1 teaspoon soy sauce

freshly ground black pepper

Garnish

2-3 tomatoes, sliced

shredded basil leaves

Preheat the oven to 200°C (400°F), Gas Mark 6. Melt the butter in a saucepan, add the garlic, stir in the breadcrumbs and cook until crisp. Remove from the heat and add the cheese, with black pepper to taste.

Open the oysters, tipping the liquor into a bowl. Add the soured cream and soy sauce to the bowl and mix well. Remove the oysters from their shells and divide them between 8 individual gratin dishes. Spoon the soured cream mixture over the top and cover that with the cheese and breadcrumb mixture.

Bake for a maximum of 10 minutes, just long enough to brown the breadcrumbs. Serve with a garnish of sliced tomatoes sprinkled with shredded basil.

Serves 8

FORESTIÈRE OYSTERS

Use Pacific *gigas* from Whitstable for this recipe, if you can get them.

16 oysters

250 g/8 oz fresh button mushrooms (or 175 g/6 oz chanterelles for a special occasion)

25 g/1 oz unsalted butter

50 g/2 oz shallots, finely chopped

juice of ½ lemon

1 tablespoon finely chopped parsley

2 tablespoons crème fraîche

50 g/2 oz Gruyère cheese, finely grated

freshly ground black pepper

Open the oysters, reserving the liquor. Remove the oysters from their shells and arrange in a shallow flameproof serving dish. Clean the button mushrooms by wiping them with kitchen paper; chop them very finely. If using chanterelles, rinse them briefly under cold water, drain and pat dry. Chop into small pieces. Melt the butter in a frying pan, add the shallots and sauté for 1 minute. Stir in the mushrooms and lemon juice and cook for 1 minute more, then add the reserved oyster liquor with black pepper to taste. Stir in the parsley and crème fraîche.

Spoon some sauce over each oyster. Sprinkle with a little grated Gruyère. Place the dish under a preheated hot grill until the cheese bubbles. Serve at once.

Serves 2

OYSTER PIES IN VINE LEAVES

Eight little pies to serve for a supper party or as a starter for 4. Use Pacific (*gigas*) oysters. Drained, blanched spinach leaves may be substituted for the vine leaves if preferred.

8 x 100-140 g/3½-4½ oz oysters

8 vine leaves

175 g/6 oz puff pastry, thawed if frozen

100 g/3½ oz butter, softened

65 g/2½ oz fresh white breadcrumbs

grated rind and juice of ½ lemon

2 tablespoons dry sherry

1 garlic clove, crushed

pinch of mace

beaten egg yolk, to glaze

Preheat the oven to 200°C (400°F), Gas Mark 6. Open the oysters, reserving the liquor. Remove the oysters from their shell. Wash and steam or blanch fresh vine leaves until tender; if using vine leaves in brine, rinse them and gently pat them dry to remove any excess water. Wrap each oyster in a vine leaf to make a small neat parcel. Set aside.

On a lightly floured surface, roll out the puff pastry and use it to line 8 small greased (mince pie) tins, reserving sufficient pastry for 8 lids.

In a bowl, mix the softened butter with the breadcrumbs, lemon rind and juice, sherry, garlic and mace. Add the reserved oyster liquor. Divide the mixture between the pastry-lined pie tins, top each with a wrapped oyster and seal with a pastry lid. Brush each pie with a little of the beaten egg yolk, make 2 small slits in the lid to allow the steam to escape and bake for 10 minutes only. Serve immediately.

Serves 4

CARPETBAG STEAK FOR THE BARBECUE

4 rump steaks, about 175 g/6 oz each

16 small, sweet oysters

50 g/2 oz butter, softened

2 garlic cloves, crushed

2 tablespoons finely chopped parsley

freshly ground black pepper

Using a good sharp knife, slit each steak lengthways to form a 'pocket'. Open the oysters, reserving the liquor for use in another recipe. In a bowl, mix the oysters with the butter, garlic and parsley.

Add pepper to taste.

Divide the oyster mixture evenly between the pockets in the steak. Close the openings with half a wooden kebab stick or metal skewer. Cook each steak on a lightly oiled barbecue; grill for the length of time that suits individual tastes.

Serves 4

Oysters are the richest animal source
                        of vitamins and minerals.

JIFFY OYSTER FEAST

4 litre/7 pint container of oyster meat in its own liquor

½ bottle dry white wine

1.5 kg/3 lb cooked peeled prawns, thawed if frozen

175 ml/6 fl oz dry sherry

a few black olives, to garnish

Saffron Rice

10 saffron threads

250 ml/8 fl oz boiling water

4 tablespoons olive oil

1 onion, about 175 g/6 oz, finely chopped

2 garlic cloves, crushed

500 g/1 lb arborio rice

900 ml/1½ pints fish stock

freshly ground black pepper

For the rice, pound the saffron to a powder. Stir in the water and set aside. Heat the oil in a pan, add the onion and garlic and sauté until translucent. Add the rice and stir until coated. Pour in the stock and saffron liquid. Bring to the boil, stir and cover. Cook for 30 minutes or until the rice is cooked. Meanwhile drain the oysters, tipping the liquor into a pan. Add the wine and bring to the boil, then simmer and add the prawns. Cook for 2 minutes. Add the oysters and cook for 1 minute more. Remove the seafood. Bring the seafood liquid back to the boil and reduce by half. Remove from the heat and stir in the sherry and season with pepper. Fork the seafood into the warm rice and pour over the sherry-flavoured liquid. Garnish with olives.

Serves 12 (or fewer)

Burlington Arcade in London was built by Lord Cavendish, former owner of Burlington House. The Arcade was built to stop passers-by from throwing their oyster shells into his garden.

OYSTERS ON TOAST

Use Pacific (*gigas*) oysters for this recipe, not the native *ostrea edulis* or the Belon, which it would be sacrilege to cook.

oysters, as many as you like

25-40 g/1-1½ oz unsalted butter, per 12 oyster

2 slices of bread, or more or less as desired

lemon wedges (optional)

Open the oysters, reserving the liquor. Melt the butter in a frying pan and toss in the oysters. Stir-fry for no more than 40 seconds, depending on the size of the oysters. Do not overcook.

Toast the bread. Using a slotted spoon, remove the oysters from the pan and pile them on to the toast.

Pour the reserved oyster liquor into the pan, swirling it into the butter. Pour over the oysters and enjoy.

A lemon wedge adds a little extra *je ne sais quoi*, but it is the perfect compliment to any oysters.

Serves 1

Caesar: **I found the British oyster**.

Apollodorus: **All posterity will bless you for it**.

George Bernard Shaw *Caesar and Cleopatra*

LOUISIANA OYSTERS

8 large oysters, about 100-140 g/3½-4½ oz each

4 rashers of rindless back bacon, chopped

I small onion, finely chopped

50 g/2 oz red pepper, deseeded and finely chopped

2 celery sticks, finely sliced

juice of I lemon

generous dash of Tabasco sauce, or to taste

salt and pepper

Preheat the oven to 160°C (325°F), Gas Mark 3. Open the oysters, reserving the liquor. Remove the oysters and arrange them in a nonstick baking dish. Set aside.

Heat the bacon in a frying pan until the fat runs, then raise the heat and fry until crispy. Add the onion, pepper and celery and cook until the vegetables are tender. Stir in the lemon juice, Tabasco and reserved oyster liquor, with salt and pepper to taste. Mix well.

Spread the mixture over the oysters and bake for 8-10 minutes or until the oysters are just cooked and begin to curl. Serve at once.

Serves 2

EASY OYSTER PIE

Make this pie in moments, using prepared puff pastry. The best oysters to use are *crassostreas*.

butter, for greasing

36 oysters

8 rashers of rindless streaky bacon

1-2 tablespoons oil

1 large onion, chopped

175 g/6 oz mushrooms, sliced

1 red pepper, deseeded and sliced or chopped

50 g/2 oz plain flour

pinch of salt

pinch of cayenne pepper

4 tablespoons chopped parsley

250 g/8 oz puff pastry, thawed if frozen

Preheat the oven to 200°C (400°F), Gas Mark 6. Grease a 1.2 litre/2 pint pie dish with the butter. Open the oysters, reserving the liquor. Remove the oysters and pat dry. Heat the bacon in a pan until the fat runs, then raise the heat and fry until crispy. Remove from the pan and chop roughly. Set aside.

Add the oil to the bacon fat remaining in the pan. When hot, add the onion, mushrooms and pepper. Toss to coat in the fat, then cover the pan and simmer the vegetables for about 5 minutes. Stir in the flour, with salt and cayenne to taste, and add the reserved oyster liquor. After a few turns with a wooden spoon, fold in the oysters and bacon with the parsley.

Pile the ingredients into the pie dish. Roll out the pastry on a lightly floured surface and cover the pie with it. Cut a cross in the top so the steam can escape. Bake for 20-25 minutes or until puffy and golden.

Serves 4-6

OYSTERS ROCKEFELLER

500 g/1lb fresh spinach or frozen

12 oysters, opened, with juice reserved

50 g/2 oz finely chopped shallots

2 garlic cloves, crushed

25g/1 oz unsalted butter

1 heaped tablespoon thick cream

1 tablespoon Pernod

pinch of hot red pepper-flakes or ½ teaspoon hot pepper sauce

50 g/2 oz grated Gruyère cheese

freshly ground black pepper

Wash the fresh spinach and place in a large saucepanwith just the water which adheres to the leaves. Heat gently for 3-4 minutes until just wilted, drain well and squeeze out the liquid. Follow the packet instructions for frozen spinach. Chop finely. Arrange the oysters on a flat, nonstick baking dish. Sauté the shallots and garlic in the butter, add the spinach, oyster juice and pepper. Add the cream and bring to a simmer. Purée the mixture in a blender. Return to a clean pan. Add the Pernod and pepper flakes (or sauce). Heat gently, to warm, stirring occasionally.

Spoon the mixture over each oyster and then sprinkle with the cheese. Place under a hot grill until the cheese sizzles, about 2 to 3 minutes. Serve immediately with whatever you choose, tiny pasta shells go well.

Serves 2

"Why, then the world's mine oyster
Which I with sword will open."

Shakespeare *The Merry Wives of Windsor*

OYSTERS WITH SPINACH AND CAVA SAUCE

Cava - the Spanish answer to champagne - makes a superb sauce. If unavailable, use a good quality
sparkling wine as a substitute.

500 g/1 lb fresh or frozen spinach

150 ml/¼ pint Cava

2 shallots, finely chopped

150 ml/¼ pint double cream

24 Pacific (*gigas*) oysters

salt and pepper

finely chopped parsley or chives (or both), to garnish

If using fresh spinach, rinse it thoroughly several times and place it in a saucepan with just the water that
adheres to the leaves. Cover the pan and cook the spinach until just tender, then drain thoroughly and
chop finely. Cook frozen spinach according to the instructions on the packet; drain well.

Keep the spinach hot.

Heat the Cava in a deep frying pan until simmering. Add the shallots to the pan and simmer for 3 minutes,
then stir in the cream and reduce the liquid by half. Add salt and pepper to taste.

Open the oysters carefully, adding the liquor to the sauce. Set the oysters aside and scrub the bottom
shells. Bring a saucepan of water to the boil, add the bottom shells and boil for 10 minutes. Drain the
shells and arrange on 4 ovenproof dishes.

Divide the spinach equally between the shells, top with the oysters and cover with the sauce. Place under
a hot grill for 1 minute until the sauce bubbles. Garnish with parsley or chives and serve immediately
with any remaining Cava sauce.

Serves 4

OYSTERS ROLAND JÖHRI - THE PASTA

This is an unusual type of pasta and is truly delicious. If you decide to use quark try to find one with 0.2% fat or a maximum of 3-4% fat so that your pasta forms a manageable dough.

150 g/5 oz plain flour, sifted

75 g/3 oz quark, fromage frais or ricotta

1 egg, beaten

2 tablespoons melted butter

To make the pasta, place the flour in a bowl, make a well in the centre and add the quark, fromage frais or ricotta, with the egg and melted butter. Gradually incorporate the flour and mix to a dough, then cover and set aside in the refrigerator for 30 minutes.

Bring a large saucepan of lightly salted water to the boil. Shave the pasta dough in thin strips directly into the boiling water. Cook for 2 minutes only, then drain thoroughly and keep hot.

Shucked oyster meat is sold in 2 litre/ 3½ pint containers in Louisiana, because they have such an abundant supply of oysters all year round. Packed in their own juice and well iced, these oysters will keep under refrigeration for at least 10 days - ideal for the cook who finds it difficult to open oysters, and a big bonus when unexpected guests arrive.

INDEX

angels on horseback, 26
aphrodisiacs, 10
au naturel oysters, 25

bacon: angels on
  horseback, 26
  easy oyster pie, 58
  Louisiana oysters, 56
baked oysters Australian
  style, 45
Bannow Bay oysters, 15
barley salad with oysters, 40
beef: beef and oyster pâté, 44
  carpetbag steak for the
  barbecue, 50
British oysters, 14-19
Burlington Arcade,
  London, 54
buying oysters, 9

canapés, oyster and
  caviar, 28
Carew oysters, 18
carpetbag steak for the
  barbecue, 50
Carroll, Lewis, 26
Cava: oysters with spinach
  and Cava sauce, 62
Cavendish, Lord, 54
caviar and oyster canapés, 28
champagne, 23
cheese: baked oysters
  Australian style, 45
  forestière oysters, 46
chillies: chilli grilled oysters
  Mexico way, 42
chilli sauce, 25

chips, oyster, 33
chowder, oyster, 30
Colchester oysters, 15
Cole, Nat King, 49
crassostrea, 7; 9

Dorset oysters, 14
drinks, 23

easy oyster pie, 58

forestière oysters, 46
freezing oysters, 25
fromage frais: pasta for
  oysters Roland Jöhri, 63

Guinness and oyster soup, 32

Helford oysters, 15
history, 11
huîtres creuses, 14

Islay oysters, 17

Jersey oysters, 14
jiffy oyster feast, 52

Loch Fyne oysters, 16
Louisiana oysters, 56, 63

mignonette sauce, 25
mushrooms: easy oyster
  pie, 58
  forestière oysters, 46

nutrition, 10 -11

Olympia oyster, 7
opening oysters, 9
Orkney Seafayre oysters, 19

ostrea edulis, 7; 9

pasta: for oysters Roland
  Jöhri, 38; 63
pâté, oyster and beef, 44
pies: easy oyster pie, 58
  oyster pies in vine leaves, 48
poacher's breakfast, 26
prawns: jiffy oyster feast, 52
pumpkin and oyster
  soufflés, 36

quark: pasta for oysters
  Roland Jöhri, 63

rice: jiffy oyster feast, 52
ricotta: pasta for oysters
  Roland Jöhri, 63
Rockefeller oysters, 60
Roland Jöhri oysters, 38
Rossmore Irish oysters, 19

saffron: jiffy oyster feast, 52
salad, barley, with oysters, 40
salmon, marinated oysters
  and, 34
sauces, 25
Seacroft oysters, 18
Seasalter Shellfish, 17
serving oysters, 20
Shakespeare, William, 60
Shaw, George Bernard, 56
shucked oyster meat, 63
soufflés, oyster and
  pumpkin, 36
soups: oyster and
  Guinness, 32
  oyster chowder, 30
species, 7
spinach: oysters Rockefeller, 60

oysters with spinach and Cava
  sauce, 62

toast, oysters on, 54

vine leaves, oyster pies in, 48

West Mersea oysters, 16
Whitstable oysters, 17
wine, 23
  oysters with spinach and Cava
  sauce, 62

**Publishers
acknowledgements**
The publishers would like to
thank the following oyster
farms, fishmongers, people
and organisations for their
invaluable help :
Neil Duncan, Seacroft Oysters,
David Hugh-Jones, Atlantic
Shellfish, B & B Fisheries,
Loch Fyne Oysters Ltd.,
Duncan Geddes, Orkney
Seafayre Oysters, Giselle
Stroud, Seasalter Shellfish,
Islay Oysters, Carew Oysters,
Ross Lee, Bannow Bay
Fisheries, Nancy Griffen,
Chris Nelson, Bon Secour
Fisheries, Bob Wallace,
Billingsgate Fish Company,
Taylor United Inc.